# MARY SHELLEY

Mary was born in London on 30 August 1797. Her father was the philosopher and novelist William Godwin. Her mother, the early women's rights campaigner Mary Wollstonecraft, died eleven days after the birth. Godwin remarried and ensured his daughter had a good education, inviting literary figures to the house such as Charles Lamb, Samuel Taylor Coleridge and, in 1812, Percy Bysshe Shelley. Already married, the poet's libertarian attitudes allowed his eyes to wander, and two years later he and sixteen-year-old Mary eloped, embarking on a European tour. William Godwin, himself a permissive man, nevertheless disapproved of this relationship. Mary gave birth prematurely to a daughter in February 1815. The baby died after two weeks and Mary wrote in her journal that she had dreamt 'my little baby came to life again; it had only been cold; we rubbed it before the fire, and it lived'. A son, William Shelley, was born the following year and lived to the age of three.

Returning to London, the couple had an 'open' relationship, each conducting affairs. Two further children were born. After Shelley's wife, Harriet, drowned herself in the Serpentine in November 1816, he and Mary married on December 30th.

In 1816, during a very wet summer holiday beside Lake Geneva, Lord Byron suggested to Shelley, Mary and a friend, George Gordon, that each attempt to write a ghost story. Mary, aged seventeen, started on *Frankenstein*. It was not finished until the summer of 1817, and was published anonymously in January 1818, to popular but mixed critical success.

Percy Bysshe Shelley drowned in the Gulf of Spezia, Italy, in summer of 1822, and Mary returned to London with her only surviving child, Percy Florence. She did not remarry, but wrote the novels *Matilda* (1819), *Valperga* (1823), *The Last Man* (1826), *Perkin Warbeck* (1830), *Lodore* (1835) and *Falkner* (1837). None was as successful as *Frankenstein*. She died in Chester Square, London, on 1 February 1851.

## PATRICK SANDFORD

Patrick Sandford is the Artistic Director of the Nuffield Theatre, Southampton. He was previously Artistic Director at the Lyric Theatre, Belfast. His adaptations include Jules Verne's *Around the World in Eighty Days*, Rudyard Kipling's *The Jungle Book*, Robert Louis Stephenson's *Treasure Island* and Kenneth Grahame's *The Wind in the Willows* – most recently performed at Derby Live. He translated *Beach Wedding* from the French *Noces de Sable* by Didier Van Cauwelaert.

As a director, his productions have been seen in Australia, France, Germany, in the West End and on the fringe in London, as well as across Britain and Ireland. He won the TMA Award for Best Director for his productions of *Much Ado About Nothing* and *The Winter Wife* by Claire Tomalin.

Mary Shelley's

# FRANKENSTEIN

*selected and structured for the stage by*

Patrick Sandford

## NICK HERN BOOKS

London
www.nickhernbooks.co.uk

**A Nick Hern Book**

This stage adaptation of *Frankenstein* first published in Great Britain as a paperback original in 2011 by Nick Hern Books Limited, The Glasshouse, 49a Goldhawk Road, London W12 8QP

Reprinted 2013

Cover image of the original 2004 production of this adaptation
© Mike Eddowes (www.theatre-photography.co.uk)
Cover designed by Ned Hoste, 2H

Typeset by Nick Hern Books, London
Printed in Great Britain by Mimeo Ltd, Cambridgeshire PE29 6XX

A CIP catalogue record for this book is available from the British Library

ISBN   978 1 84842 194 3

**Production Note**

Mary Shelley's original has been considerably distorted by film versions.

In her book the chief characteristics of Frankenstein are pride followed by regret.

The Creature is highly intelligent, physically powerful and emotionally vulnerable. He need not necessarily be naked. In the original production he was swathed in wet muslin, and later dressed in clothes stolen from Frankenstein's university room.

Clearly the body parts cannot be real. A lateral interpretation must be found. In the original production a group of real hands pushed through the floor trickling earth and holding human organs. Other solutions might involve Victorian encyclopedia etchings of human limbs, or projections of funerary statuary. Directors and designers will have better ideas.

The original design was fluid, suiting the fast-moving 'story within a story' structure of the play, hinting at locations rather than representing them literally.

**Textual Note**

The words of this play are taken almost entirely from the 1818 edition of Mary Shelley's novel, with one short passage from the revised 1831 edition.

The quotations from Percy Bysshe Shelley and Samuel Taylor Coleridge are included by Mary Shelley. The abbreviated fable of Jean de la Fontaine is referred to by Mary Shelley.

The language, educated and sometimes formal, should be spoken simply and swiftly. Elisions (e.g. 'haven't' for 'have not') should happen quite naturally.

Stage directions from the original production are in italics and may of course be ignored. Some of these reflect directly Mary Shelley's wording.

This stage adaptation of *Frankenstein* was first performed at the Nuffield Theatre, Southampton on 22 September 2004, with the following cast:

| | |
|---|---|
| VICTOR FRANKENSTEIN | Ben Porter |
| THE CREATURE | Max Digby |
| CAPTAIN WALTON / | Adam Farr |
| HENRY CLERVAL / FELIX | |
| FATHER / OLD MAN | William Whymper |
| ELIZABETH / SAFIE | Lisa McNaught |
| WILLIAM | Nathan Hack / |
| | Harry Sykes / Simon Paul |
| JUSTINE | Jess Farnhill / Helen Jolley |
| | Becky Pennick |
| AGATHA | Mel Kitcher / Natalie Sahota |
| | Olivia Smith |

*A chorus of people drawn from the community played the ship's crew, scientists and townspeople*

| | |
|---|---|
| *Director* | Patrick Sandford |
| *Designer* | Robin Don |
| *Lighting Designer* | David W Kidd |
| *Composer* | Simon Slater |
| *Community Director* | Fran Morley |

**Characters**

*in order of appearance*

CAPTAIN WALTON, *a polar explorer*
VICTOR FRANKENSTEIN
ELIZABETH, *Frankenstein's cousin*
HENRY CLERVAL, *Frankenstein's friend*
FATHER, *to Frankenstein*
WILLIAM, *Frankenstein's little brother, aged seven or eight*
JUSTINE, *William's young nurse*
THE CREATURE
OLD MAN
FELIX, *a peasant*
AGATHA, *a young peasant girl, perhaps fourteen or fifteen*
SAFIE, *a young Turkish woman*

*Plus Arctic crewmen, scientists, villagers, a hangman,
townspeople*

*Before the play, the image, by whatever means, of a disembodied arm – female – writing.*

## ACT ONE

### Scene One

*The play begins and ends on the ice.*

*Out of the darkness a face appears, tightly lit. It is* CAPTAIN WALTON, *a young polar explorer.*

WALTON. There is something at work in my soul which I don't understand – a love for the marvellous, a belief in the marvellous! This hurries me out of the common pathways of men, even to the mysteries of the ocean. I am going to the land of mist and snow, never before imprinted by the foot of man, surpassing in wonders and beauty every region discovered on the globe. These enticements conquer all fear of danger or death. My daydreams are extended and magnificent!

*Light builds to reveal the ship's* CREW *in Arctic clothing. Activity.*

But I have one want which I have never yet been able to satisfy: I have no friend. When I am glowing with success, there will be no one to participate in my joy; if I am assailed by disappointment, no one to sustain me. I greatly need the company of a man with the sense not to despise me as romantic, whose eyes will reply to mine.

Well, I shall certainly find no such friend on the wide ocean.

I shall do nothing rashly. I shall kill no albatross, nor return woeful as the Ancient Mariner. Success shall crown my endeavours, the stars witnessing my triumph! What can stop the determined heart and resolved will of man?

*Violent storm then silence.*

*The* CREW *stand motionless in the mist.*

*(Drily.)* The winter has been dreadfully severe.

CREWMAN *(nearly hostile).* Ice-bound. Shut in on all sides. Vast plains which seem to have no end.

*Silence then distant barking.*

LOOKOUT. Sledge!

*Distant cry. All strain to see, some with telescopes.*

*Behind them an arm, unseen and in distress, slowly appears through the stage. Nobody sees it. It subsides.*

*The* CREW *drag on the sledge bearing* VICTOR FRANKENSTEIN.

WALTON. I never saw a man in so wretched a condition.

Friend…

FRANKENSTEIN. Captain, before I board your vessel, will you have the kindness to inform me whither you are bound?

WALTON. Towards the Northern Pole, where the sun is forever visible. We are on a voyage of discovery.

FRANKENSTEIN *laughs bitterly. The laugh seizes him as time passes and he is lifted from the sledge, blanketed and installed comfortably, perhaps in a hammock or berth, facing* WALTON.

I am to discover a passage near the Pole to countries as yet inaccessible, and also the secret of magnetism, the wondrous power which attracts the needle. Sir, you cannot contest the benefit I shall confer on mankind…

FRANKENSTEIN. Unhappy man! So you share my madness. Have you drunk of the intoxicating draught? Let me reveal my tale, and you will dash the cup from your lips!

WALTON. Why have you come so far upon the ice?

FRANKENSTEIN. I seek one who flees from me.

WALTON. And does this man travel in the same fashion?

FRANKENSTEIN. Yes.

WALTON. Then I fancy we have seen him; for this very night we saw dogs drawing a sledge across the ice, with a man in it, of gigantic [*Meaning powerful.*] stature.

FRANKENSTEIN. His route?

WALTON. North.

FRANKENSTEIN. Do you think the ice cracking could have destroyed his sledge?

WALTON. The ice didn't break until nearly midnight. He might have arrived at a place of safety before then.

FRANKENSTEIN *is very anxious.*

I promise someone will watch for him, and give you instant notice of any new sighting.

FRANKENSTEIN. Doubtless, Captain, I have excited your curiosity, as well as that of these good people...

WALTON. It would be impertinent to trouble you with inquisitiveness.

FRANKENSTEIN. Yet you have rescued me from a perilous situation and benevolently restored me to life.

WALTON. Friend...

FRANKENSTEIN (*immediately pained*). I once had a friend, the most noble of men, and I am entitled, therefore, to judge respecting friendship. You have hope, and the world before you. But I have lost everything, and cannot begin anew.

You seek for knowledge as once I did and I hope the gratification of your wishes may not be a serpent to sting you, as I was stung. You may deduce a moral from my tale; one to direct you if you succeed, and console you in case of failure. Prepare to hear of such occurrences... (*He shudders.*) I might fear your disbelief, even your ridicule; but in these wild and mysterious regions many things will seem possible.

WALTON. I cannot request that you renew your grief by reciting...

FRANKENSTEIN. Thank you for your sympathy, but it is useless; my fate is sealed. I wait for one event, and then I shall rest in peace. My friend, if thus you will allow me to name you, nothing can alter my destiny. Listen to my history, and you will see how irrevocably it is determined.

*The* CREW *draws close.*

WALTON. Strange and harrowing must be his story; frightful the storm which embraced this gallant vessel, and wrecked it – thus!

*Lights change.*

VOICE OF ELIZABETH. William! William!

FRANKENSTEIN *removes his Arctic coat and is revealed as a young man.*

### Scene Two

*Geneva.*

*Sunshine. A picnic.*

*Enter St George (played by* HENRY CLERVAL*) and a dragon. They are watched by a benevolent* FATHER *carrying on his shoulders a child (*WILLIAM*), who squeals in delight. George slays the dragon.*

FRANKENSTEIN *is immersed in his books.*

FATHER. Victor!

JUSTINE. Victor!

HENRY. VICTOR!!!

*The dragon splits in two – the back half is* JUSTINE*, the maid, who gathers up* WILLIAM*.*

FRANKENSTEIN. Hello, Henry... Hello, Elizabeth.

*The dragon takes its head off. It is* ELIZABETH. HENRY *lifts a specimen jar containing some spongy thing.*

ELIZABETH. What's that?

HENRY. Ugh!

FRANKENSTEIN. Friends. Dear friends. The world to me is a secret which I desire to discover. To you it is a vacancy which you seek to people with imaginations of your own.

ELIZABETH *tickles him.*

FATHER. Victor, don't forget it was your mother's final wish to see your future happiness in union with Elizabeth...

FRANKENSTEIN. My cousin! My more than sister!

FATHER....and I never saw such grace both of person and mind; a gentle and affectionate disposition, playful as a summer insect, eyes lively as a bird. Her look sheds radiance.

HENRY. Everyone adores Elizabeth.

FRANKENSTEIN *and* ELIZABETH *kiss. It is clear she loves him.*

FATHER (*looking at the books*). What! Cornelius Agrippa, *On Occult Philosophy*! Victor, don't waste your time.

FRANKENSTEIN. But, Father, the wonderful things he relates, and the theory he attempts to demonstrate...

FATHER. Sad trash! You will do better at the university. Here in Geneva we are dull. We are dull!

HENRY (*singing with gruesome relish*).
    On the study table a book there lay,
    Which Agrippa had been writing that day.
    The letters were written with blood therein,
    And the pages were made of dead men's skin.
    The young man saw in the pages between,
    The ugliest pictures that ever were seen,
    The likeness of things so foul to behold,
    That what they were is not fit to be told.

ELIZABETH. Stop it.

HENRY. The conjuror's eyes red fury dart,
  And out he tore the young man's heart.
  He grinn'd a horrible grin at his prey,
  And in a clap of thunder vanished away.
  Moral: Henceforth let all young men take heed,
  How in a conjuror's books they read!

ELIZABETH. Henry.

HENRY. Oh, Victor! I wish I was coming to Ingolstadt with you. My father believes universities are superfluous in ordinary life.

ELIZABETH. Cornelius Agrippa. Victor, it's ancient!

FRANKENSTEIN. The original physical sciences, Elizabeth. The secrets that I know, I just know, will regulate my fate.

*They peruse the books.*

HENRY. *Paracelsus Bombastus!*

ELIZABETH. *The Search for the Philosopher's Stone…*

FRANKENSTEIN. Pah! Wealth is an inferior object.

ELIZABETH. *…and the Elixir of Life.*

FRANKENSTEIN. Life! Elizabeth. Life!

ELIZABETH. Victor…

FRANKENSTEIN. My mother is dead, Elizabeth. I need not describe the void that presents. It's so long before the mind can persuade itself that she, who we saw every day, and whose very existence seemed part of our own, can have departed for ever – that the brightness of her eye can have been extinguished, and the sound of a voice so dear to the ear can be hushed, nevermore to be heard.

FATHER. Peace, Victor.

ELIZABETH. You describe a sorrow we have all felt, all must feel. But we must still continue our course. We must still endeavour to contribute to the happiness of others.

HENRY. Elizabeth renews the spirit of cheerfulness in our little society.

FRANKENSTEIN. But imagine, Elizabeth! Imagine! If I could banish disease and death from the human frame. What discovery! What glory!

ELIZABETH. Victor...

FRANKENSTEIN. Why not? There are natural phenomena that take place every day before our eyes.

*The picnic kettle boils.* FRANKENSTEIN *takes* ELIZABETH *by the hand.*

Come here. Wait, Justine...

HENRY. Look, everybody!

WILLIAM *wants to get close to the kettle.*

FATHER. Be careful, William.

FRANKENSTEIN (*demonstrating with a piece of glass or a saucer*). Distillation, and the wondrous effects of steam.

*He throws open the hamper lid. A balloon floats upwards with a wire cable.* WILLIAM *is ecstatic.*

Experiment on the lightness of air and other gases.

*Lightning and a distant rumble of thunder.*

And what is the origin of thunder and lightning?

*They wait.* FATHER *shakes his head.*

Electricity, Father... Electricity. Fluid from the clouds!

*The electricity travels down the wire.*

*Thunder. Rain. Umbrellas.*

FATHER (*calling as they exit*). Bless you, Victor.

HENRY. Write often, Victor!

FRANKENSTEIN *and* ELIZABETH *are alone and close.*

FRANKENSTEIN. I ardently desire the acquisition of knowledge. It is so hard to remain cooped up in one place. I long to enter the world, and take my station among other human beings.

*Lights change.*

**Scene Three**

*University.*

FRANKENSTEIN, *alone. From this point he will increasingly address the audience directly.*

*Enter a flock of university* SCIENTISTS, *perhaps white periwigged, white frock-coated. They surround* FRANKENSTEIN.

FRANKENSTEIN *has papers and his journal. He works.*

FRANKENSTEIN. I feel as if one by one the very keys of my soul are being touched, chord after chord is sounded, and my mind is filled with one thought, one conception, one purpose. So much has been done — more, far more, will I achieve.

ELIZABETH. Victor!

*She calls as from a great distance. She cannot reach him.*

FRANKENSTEIN. My being is in a state of insurrection!

HENRY. Victor?

FRANKENSTEIN *shuts himself in and the world out.*

FRANKENSTEIN. None but those who have experienced them can conceive of the enticements of science. In other subjects you go as far as others have gone before you, and there is nothing more to know; but in a scientific pursuit there is continual discovery and wonder.

One of the phenomena which has peculiarly attracted my attention is the structure of the human frame, indeed, any animal endued with life. From where does the principle of life proceed?

In this enlightened and scientific age... to examine the causes of life... we must first have recourse to... death.

(*Thinking it through.*) The science of anatomy is not sufficient. I must also observe the natural decay and corruption of the dead human body.

There is no distaste. In my education my father took precautions that my mind should be impressed with no supernatural horrors. I have never trembled at a tale of darkness or superstition; a churchyard is to me merely the receptacle of bodies deprived of life. I must spend days and nights in vaults and charnel houses.

*Music.*

*Perhaps the suggestion of death.*

I must examine the progress of this decay. I must see how the fine form of man is degraded and wasted. I must behold the corruption of death succeed the blooming of life; how the worm inherits the wonders of the eye and brain. I must examine and analyse all the minutiae of the change from life to death –

*For* FRANKENSTEIN, *a penny begins to drop.*

And from death to life.

From death to life.

Until... Until...

*He works, intensely, feverishly, but with absolute control.*

*He reviews what he has written in his journal.*

Until a light breaks in upon me.
A light so brilliant and wondrous.
Yet so simple.

I grow dizzy with the immensity of the prospect it illustrates. Can it be, among so many men of genius determined on the same quest, that I alone should discover so astonishing a secret?

*His arrogance grows.*

This is not the vision of a madman. The sun does not shine in the heavens more certainly than the truth of what I affirm. I have succeeded in discovering the cause of generation and life. Nay more, I am certain, beyond doubt, that I am now capable of bestowing animation upon lifeless matter.

*He turns to the audience coldly.*

I see by your eagerness, and the wonder and hope which your eyes express, that you expect to be informed of the secret.

*He shakes his head.*

That cannot be.

ELIZABETH. Victor!

FATHER *and* HENRY. Victor!

*But they cannot reach him…*

FRANKENSTEIN. How shall I employ so astonishing a power? I possess the capacity of bestowing animation! But to prepare a frame for the reception of it, with all the intricacies of fibres, muscles, and veins. This remains a work of inconceivable difficulty and labour.

I have no doubt of my ability. My imagination is vivid; my powers of analysis are intense; and I possess a coolness of judgement that fits me for achievement. I would deem it criminal to throw away these talents. I cannot rank myself with the herd.

I will pioneer a new way, explore unknown powers, and unfold to the world the deepest mysteries of creation.

Life and death appear to me ideal bounds, which I shall be the first to break through, pouring a torrent of light into our dark world.

I, Victor Frankenstein, begin the creation of a human being.

*Music.*

FRANKENSTEIN *harvests the human organs.*

A new species will bless me as its creator; many happy and excellent natures will owe their being to me.

FATHER. Victor!

FRANKENSTEIN. No father could claim the gratitude of his child so completely as I shall deserve theirs.

*He works with great assurance.*

ELIZABETH. The summer months pass; a most beautiful season full of the charms of nature; the blossom and the expanding leaves.

HENRY. Never did the fields bestow a more plentiful harvest, or the vines yield a more luxuriant vintage.

ELIZABETH (*close to tears*). I know that you will think of us with affection, Victor. I know we shall hear regularly from you.

FRANKENSTEIN. I select his features as beautiful. His limbs will be in proportion.

FATHER. A human being in perfection ought always to preserve a peaceful spirit. The pursuit of knowledge is no exception to this rule. If the study to which you apply yourself has a tendency to weaken your affections, and to destroy your taste for simple pleasures, then that study is not befitting the human mind.

ELIZABETH. Victor! Victor!

*It snows finely on the family.*

FRANKENSTEIN (*savagely*). If this rule were always observed; if no man allowed any pursuit to interfere with the tranquillity of his domestic affections, Julius Caesar would have failed his country. America would not have been discovered.

*He is poised at the final moment of the experiment.*

HENRY. It is a dreary night of November.

ELIZABETH. The leaves of the year are withering.

*She is in grief.*

FRANKENSTEIN. Beautiful. Beautiful.

*The ice splits.*

*The* CREATURE *is 'born'. We do not see its face.*

So beautiful!

*Silence or the gentle splashing of water.*

*Slowly* FRANKENSTEIN*'s expression changes.*

I have worked so hard. I have worked so hard. I have deprived myself of rest and health. My cheek has grown pale with study, and my body emaciated with confinement. My limbs still tremble and my eyes swim. Sometimes on the very brink of certainty I failed, yet always I clung to hope. But now the dream that has been my food is become a hell. The beauty is vanished.

(*Pointing.*) No mortal could support the horror of that countenance. A thing such as even Dante could not have conceived. I cannot endure the aspect.

*He leaves to vomit.*

*The* CREATURE *is motionless.*

*It is still snowing.*

*Slowly the* CREATURE *stretches out his hand to feel the snowflakes, like a child. The moon rises. He is fearful then enchanted.*

*Tentatively he explores his world.*

*Lights change.*

## Scene Four

FRANKENSTEIN *returns. The* CREATURE *has disappeared.*
FRANKENSTEIN *searches for him in terror. He sees light
beneath a door or from the wings. He approaches...*

*But it is* HENRY *and* SCIENTISTS.

HENRY. My dear Frankenstein. How glad I am to see you. At
last my father has permitted me a voyage to this land of
learning!

FRANKENSTEIN (*numb*). It gives me the greatest delight to
see you.

SCIENTIST. Damn this youngster Frankenstein! Why, Mr
Clerval, I assure you he has outstripped us all. Quite
astonishing progress in the sciences. If he is not soon pulled
down a peg, we shall all be out of countenance.

FRANKENSTEIN *tries to escape them.*

Aha! Mr Frankenstein is modest; an excellent quality in a
young man... And secret. Ssh! None so secret as Mr
Frankenstein.

*The* SCIENTISTS *have gone.*

HENRY. Victor, how very ill you look; so thin and pale; as if
you had not slept for nights.

FRANKENSTEIN. You have guessed right, Henry; I have been
so deeply engaged in work I have not allowed myself rest,
but I hope, I sincerely hope, that all these employments are
now at an end, and that I am at last free. I am free. I am free.
I am free!

*He laughs hysterically.*

HENRY. Victor, what, for God's sake, is the matter? Why do
you laugh in that manner? What is the cause of all this?

FRANKENSTEIN. Do not ask me. 'He' can tell. Oh, save me! Save me! A mummy endued with animation could not be so hideous.

*He is hallucinating.*

> Like one who, on a lonely road,
> Doth walk in fear and dread,
> And, having once turned round, walks on,
> And turns no more his head;
> Because he knows a frightful fiend,
> Doth close behind him tread!

HENRY. In reality you are very ill indeed. (*Starts to tend to him.*)

FRANKENSTEIN. Dearest Henry, how kind you are to me. How shall I ever repay you?

HENRY. You will repay me entirely by not discomposing yourself, and getting well as fast as you can.

FRANKENSTEIN. Forgive me. Forgive me. I feel the greatest remorse...

HENRY. Shh!

*He cradles* FRANKENSTEIN *and rattles on cheerily.*

You may easily believe the difficulty I had persuading my father to allow me to come. His constant answer was the same as the schoolmaster's in *The Vicar of Wakefield* – 'Latin and Greek? Pah! I have ten thousand a year without Latin and Greek, I eat heartily without Latin and Greek.' But his affection for me at last overcame his dislike of learning, and here I am.

FRANKENSTEIN. My favourite companion...

HENRY. Shh! But I am no natural scientist. My imagination is too vivid. Languages are my study; Latin and Greek, of course, but also Persian, Arabic, and Hebrew. I find great consolation in the Orientalists. Their joy is most elevating.

*Enter* ELIZABETH.

When you read their writings, life appears to consist in a warm sun and garden of roses, in the smiles and frowns of a fair female enemy –

ELIZABETH *sits beside* FRANKENSTEIN.

– and the fire that consumes your own heart. How different from the manly and heroic poetry of Greece and Rome...

FRANKENSTEIN *is almost asleep.*

*Lights change.*

*Enter the* CREATURE. *Only* FRANKENSTEIN *is aware of him.*

*Sudden, terrifying noise;* VILLAGERS *attack the* CREATURE.

## Scene Five

*Geneva.*

ELIZABETH....And as for gossip, Victor, they say pretty Miss Mansfield is to marry.

HENRY. *To marry*, Victor.

ELIZABETH. Yes, in the autumn, a rich banker, and your schoolfriend Louis is... well...

HENRY. *Getting engaged,* Victor.

ELIZABETH. Stop it, Henry! Louis is calling upon a very pretty –

HENRY. – very lively Frenchwoman.

ELIZABETH. Henry!

*Enter* WILLIAM (*in fancy dress as Prince Allahdin*) *and* JUSTINE.

HENRY. – and of course Prince Allahdin and the little Princess lived together in the utmost bliss!

*WILLIAM runs to FRANKENSTEIN with the magic lamp. He is wearing a miniature cameo about his neck.*

FRANKENSTEIN (*re: cameo*). This is Mother. It is her picture.

*WILLIAM runs off with JUSTINE.*

ELIZABETH. He teased me that he might wear it.

*ELIZABETH kisses FRANKENSTEIN tenderly.*

You are getting better, Victor, but you must have been exceedingly ill.

*They embrace.*

FRANKENSTEIN. You have both spent this whole winter in my sickroom. A selfish pursuit cramped and narrowed me, until your gentleness and affection warmed and opened my senses. You have taught me to love the world again –

*He returns ELIZABETH's kiss, realising what he has.*

– and the cheerful faces of children. William, for example!

ELIZABETH. He is grown very tall for his age, and when he smiles two little dimples appear on each cheek! (*Calling.*) William!

HENRY. William!

ELIZABETH. Justine?

*Alarm. ELIZABETH and HENRY exit in search.*

FATHER (*off*). William!

*FRANKENSTEIN is seized by a nightmare vision.*

*Perhaps WILLIAM runs wearing the dragon's head. JUSTINE pursues him.*

*The CREATURE seems to be everywhere.*

FRANKENSTEIN.

> Like one who, on a lonely road,
> Doth walk in fear and dread,
> And, having once turned round, walks on,
> And turns no more his head;

(*Yelling.*) William!

> Because he knows a frightful fiend,
> Doth close behind him tread!

*Perhaps the arm sinks into the floor, the hand holding the miniature cameo.*

FATHER, ELIZABETH *and* HENRY *enter with the body of* WILLIAM.

FATHER. William is dead.

FRANKENSTEIN. No.

FATHER. Your little brother, whose smiles delighted and warmed our hearts.

FRANKENSTEIN. No.

FATHER. Victor, he is murdered! I discovered my lovely boy stretched on the grass, livid and motionless; the print of the murderer's finger on his neck.

ELIZABETH. It is I who have murdered the darling child! It is I who let him wear the valuable miniature of your mother.

FATHER. Alas, Victor! I now say thank God your mother did not live to witness the cruel death of her youngest child.

HENRY. I can offer you no consolation, my friend. Your disaster is irreparable. But William is now at rest; he knows no pain.

*Exit* HENRY *and* ELIZABETH *with the body.*

FRANKENSTEIN. It is 'he'. It is 'he'. Nothing in human shape could have destroyed that fair child.

FATHER. Would it were so. But since the murderer has been discovered –

FRANKENSTEIN. The murderer discovered! Good God! How
can that be?

JUSTINE, *now in prison dress, enters slowly, followed by
the* HANGMAN *and a crowd of* TOWNSPEOPLE.

(*Appalled.*) Justine! Is she the accused? But it is wrong;
everyone must know that; no one believes it, surely, Father.

FATHER. No one did at first; but circumstances have forced
conviction upon us. The picture of your mother, judged to be
the temptation of the murderer, was discovered in her pocket.
On being charged with the fact, she confirmed the suspicion
by her extreme confusion of manner. Who would credit that
Justine, so amiable and fond of all the family, could become
so extremely wicked?

FRANKENSTEIN. You are all mistaken; I know the murderer.
Justine, poor, good Justine, is innocent.

ELIZABETH. Our misfortune is doubly hard; we have not only
lost that darling boy, but this poor young woman, whom I
sincerely love, is to be torn away by an even worse fate. If
she is condemned, I shall nevermore know joy.

FRANKENSTEIN. She is innocent, Elizabeth, innocent, and
that shall be proved.

*The* HANGMAN *puts the sack on* JUSTINE's *head.*

FATHER. I fear not, Victor, and I had rather be for ever
ignorant than have discovered so much depravity in one I
valued so highly.

*The noose is around* JUSTINE's *neck.* FRANKENSTEIN *is
desperate.*

FRANKENSTEIN. A thousand times rather let me confess
myself guilty of the crime.

FATHER. Pah! The raving of a madman. (*Fierce.*) She can give
no account of the picture. She has no power of explaining it.
We are left to conjecture how it might have been placed in
her pocket. Did the murderer place it there? She knows of no

opportunity afforded him to do so; and even if he had, why steal the jewel, to part with it again so soon?

ELIZABETH. I see no room for hope.

*As the* HANGMAN *releases the trapdoor beneath* JUSTINE'*s feet.*

FRANKENSTEIN. She is the most benevolent of human creatures!

*It is over. Silence.*

*The* CREATURE *watches.*

*Lights change.*

## Scene Six

FRANKENSTEIN, *alone.*

FRANKENSTEIN. Nothing is more painful to the human mind than the dead calm of inaction. It deprives the soul of hope. William and Justine died; they rest; and I am alive. The blood flows freely in my veins, but a weight presses on me, for I have committed mischief, horrible beyond description.

And my heart overflows. I did begin with benevolent intentions. I did thirst for the moment when I should put them into practice for my fellow beings. I *did*! Now all is blasted: guilt hurries me to hell.

*Enter* ELIZABETH.

Elizabeth...

ELIZABETH. When I reflect on these deaths, I no longer see the world as it before appeared to me. Before, I looked upon accounts of vice and injustice, that I read in books or heard from others, as tales or imaginary evils. They were remote. But now misery has come home.

Everybody believed that poor girl to be guilty. But she was
innocent. I know. When falsehood can look so like the truth,
Victor, who can be sure of happiness? Men appear to me
now as monsters thirsting for each other's blood.

FRANKENSTEIN *is distraught.*

FRANKENSTEIN. Oh, that I might plunge into the silent lake,
and the water close over my calamities for ever. Or that I
might see 'him' again, and wreak the utmost abhorrence on
his head.

ELIZABETH. Victor, calm yourself. There is an expression of
despair, and sometimes revenge, in your countenance, that
makes me tremble. Dear Victor, banish these dark passions.
Remember the friends around you, who centre all their hopes
in you, here in this land of beauty. While we love – while we
are true to each other – what can disturb our peace?

*He attempts to embrace her, but draws back, numb.*

FRANKENSTEIN. I am encompassed by a cloud, which not
the tenderness of friendship, nor the beauty of the earth can
penetrate. The very accents of love are ineffectual.

*He moves away from her.*

ELIZABETH.

> We rest. – A dream has power to poison sleep;
> We rise. – One wandering thought pollutes the day;
> We feel, conceive or reason, laugh or weep,
> Embrace fond woe, or cast our cares away:
>
> It is the same! – For, be it joy or sorrow,
> The path of its departure still is free:
> Man's yesterday may ne'er be like his morrow;
> Nothing endures but mutability. *

*Lights change.*

---

* This poem by Percy Bysshe Shelley, included by Mary Shelley, may, if
wished, be omitted in performance.

## Scene Seven

*The Alpine glacier.*

FRANKENSTEIN, *alone.*

FRANKENSTEIN. Solitude is my only consolation.

It drives me to seek relief, by bodily exercise and change of place. So I bend my steps towards the Alpine valleys. In their magnificence, their eternity, I seek to forget myself and my ephemeral, human sorrows.

I enter the valley of Chamonix. Immense glaciers approach. I hear the rumbling thunder of the falling avalanche, and mark the smoke of its passage.

The weight upon my spirit lightens. Mont Blanc, supreme and magnificent, rises, its tremendous dome towering above, as if belonging to another earth, the habitation of another race of beings.

A tingling long-lost sense of pleasure comes across me. The very winds whisper in soothing accents, and maternal nature bids me weep no more.

(*He calls out.*) Wandering spirits, if indeed ye wander, and do not rest in your narrow beds, allow me this faint happiness.

*The bleating of mountain goats.*

Alas! Why does man boast of feelings superior to those in the beast? These feelings only render us more needy. If our impulses were confined to hunger, thirst, and desire, we might very nearly be free.

I spend the day roaming. The glittering pinnacles, the ragged bare ravine; the eagle soaring amid the clouds — these scenes elevate me from all littleness of feeling; and though they do not remove my grief, they subdue and tranquillise it, and bid me be at peace.

Exhaustion succeeds. For a short space I watch the pallid lightnings play above Mont Blanc, and listen to the river pursue its noisy way beneath. The sound acts as a lullaby: sleep creeps over me; I feel it as it comes, and bless the giver of oblivion.

*He sleeps.*

### Scene Eight

*Suddenly, the* CREATURE *appears.* FRANKENSTEIN *is wide awake.*

FRANKENSTEIN. Devil! How dare you approach me? Do you not fear the fierce vengeance of my arm? Or that I might trample you to dust? Oh, that I could with your extinction restore the victims you have so diabolically murdered! Monster! Fiend!

CREATURE (*drily*). I expected this reception!

All men hate the wretched; how then must I be hated? Yet you, my creator, spurn me. You purpose to kill me. How dare you sport with life? Do your duty to me, and I will do mine to you and the rest of mankind. If you comply with my conditions, I will leave them and you at peace; but if you refuse, I will glut the maw of death until it is satiated with the blood of your companions.

FRANKENSTEIN (*goes to attack the* CREATURE). Come on, then, that I may extinguish the spark I so carelessly ignited.

*The* CREATURE *disarms him easily.*

CREATURE. Frankenstein, I am your creation. You owe me justice and clemency, and even your affection. I ought to be your Adam. Instead I am the fallen angel...

FRANKENSTEIN. Begone! I will not listen to you. There can be no community between you and me; we are enemies.

CREATURE. How can I reach your goodness? If you, my creator, abhor me, what hope can I gather? Your fellow beings arm themselves for my destruction. These glaciers and caves of ice are my sole refuge.

Listen to my tale: then abandon or commiserate me, as you judge I deserve. The guilty are allowed to speak in their defence before they are condemned. You accuse me of murder; and yet you, with a clear conscience, would murder your own creation. Oh, praise the eternal justice of man!

FRANKENSTEIN. Cursed be the day in which you first saw light! You have made me wretched beyond expression. Go! Relieve me from the sight of you.

*The* CREATURE *covers* FRANKENSTEIN*'s eyes with his hands.*

CREATURE. And so I take from you the sight which you abhor. But you can still hear me, Frankenstein, and grant me your compassion. I demand this from you. On you it rests whether I lead a harmless life, or become the scourge of your fellow creatures, and the author of your own speedy ruin. The sun is yet high in the heavens. Before it descends behind yon snowy precipice you will have heard my story, and can decide.

FRANKENSTEIN (*his eyes still closed*). My heart is full. I believe you are the murderer of my little brother. Yet for the first time, also, I feel the duties of a creator towards his creation, and that before I complain of your wickedness I ought to render you happy.

Come then: speak.

*The* CREATURE *prepares himself, throwing down papers and a book.* FRANKENSTEIN *is surprised as he realises his creation can read.*

CREATURE (*mildly indignant*). La Fontaine. The Fables.

**Scene Nine**

*The* CREATURE *tells his story. Pastoral sequence.*

CREATURE. It is difficult to remember the origin of my being. A strange multiplicity of sensations seized me. I saw, I felt, I heard and smelt at the same time. Then by degrees I remember a warm and stronger light pressed upon my nerves so I was obliged to shut my eyes.

*He does so. Sound.*

And then…

*We hear the same terrifying noise of the* VILLAGERS *attacking the* CREATURE *as before.*

They attack and grievously bruise me with stones and many other missiles. I flee and hide… And from my hiding place, a cottage pigsty, I watch the family of exiles.

*A blind* OLD MAN *enters with a stick and sits. He drowses.*

FELIX, *a peasant, drags a heavy bale of logs to the side of the stage and exits again, throwing down an axe.*

AGATHA, *a young girl, enters with bread for the* OLD MAN.

AGATHA (*calling*). Felix!

CREATURE. Fe-lix…

AGATHA *exits to look for* FELIX. *The* CREATURE *steals the bread.*

FELIX *returns and tries to move the log again. It is too heavy. He goes upstage anxiously, watching for somebody in the distance.*

*The* CREATURE *moves the log and hides again.* FELIX *turns back, he is amazed.*

FELIX. Wonderful!

CREATURE. Won-der-ful.

*AGATHA returns with a jug of milk and cheese.*

FELIX. Father. Food.

CREATURE. Father... Food...

*They eat the meagre meal. The* OLD MAN *drinks but it is not enough. He turns his head forlornly. Silently* AGATHA *and* FELIX *give him their food and drink.*

OLD MAN. Not yours.

FELIX (*lying*). No, Father, there's plenty.

CREATURE. Plen-ty.

*The* CREATURE *watches. He throws berries from his hiding place.* AGATHA *and* FELIX *are puzzled. They share the berries.*

*The* CREATURE *dispatches more supplies – perhaps turnips, cabbages, fruit, rolled joyously across the space.*

AGATHA. Look.

FELIX. Some goodly spirit!

*They eat. The* FATHER *plays on an instrument (a guitar, or zither). The* CREATURE *is enchanted.*

SAFIE (*off*). Felix!

FELIX. Safie!

AGATHA. She's here, Father.

*Enter* SAFIE, *a young, elegant Turkish woman. They embrace. She weeps for joy.*

SAFIE (*fast*). Felix, hayatim, seni ne kadar ozledim. Nihayet emniyetteyiz. [Felix, my darling. How I have missed you. At last we're safe. I love you.]

FELIX. You are safe. You are safe. Exiled, but oh, you are safe!

CREATURE. Safe.

SAFIE. Seni cuk seviyorum.

CREATURE. Se-ni-cuk...

FELIX. Shh! Safie. (*Slowly.*) This – is – my – sis-ter, –
A-ga-tha. – This – is – my – fa-ther.

SAFIE. Seester... Father... How – do – you – do?

AGATHA. How do you do?

CREATURE. Seester... Father... How – do – you – do?

FELIX (*smiling*). Bread... Milk... Wood... Father... Felix...
Sister.

   SAFIE *and the* CREATURE *repeat the words.*

   SAFIE *sings in Turkish. The* CREATURE *watches, strongly
   attracted.*

   AGATHA *brings in books. A reading lesson. The*
   CREATURE *echoes.*

   Reading!

SAFIE. The history of the world... Rome... Christianity... The
discovery of America... The unhappy fate of the natives...

   *Resisting sadness, they throw the book aside and dance, at
   first apart. A mid-European, perhaps Turkish dance. The*
   CREATURE *takes up the book and reads.*

CREATURE. The – unhappy – fate – of – the – natives... (*He
reflects bewildered.*) Man – is – powerful. But – so – cruel.
How – can – man – go – forth – to – kill – his – fellow?

   FELIX *is looking for the book. The* CREATURE, *unseen,
   returns it.*

FELIX. The division of property... Nobility and wealth...
Poverty and slavery. You, Safie, are in exile from your
country, as we are, but you are of high rank.

CREATURE (*now completely articulate but despairing*). And what am I? Who am I? Whence did I come? What is my destination? I have no friends. I am a blot upon the earth, from whom all flee.

Of what strange nature is knowledge! Once seized it clings like moss upon the rock. I wish to shake it off...

*AGATHA is asleep. FELIX and SAFIE dance closer. They look into each other's eyes. Gently erotic.*

SAFIE. And you have given up your wealth to rescue me.

FELIX. Compassion –

SAFIE *and* CREATURE. Compassion –

FELIX. Generosity –

SAFIE *and* CREATURE. Generosity –

FELIX. Love...

*They kiss. The kiss is held. The CREATURE is transfixed.*

CREATURE (*as if from a book*). The difference of the sexes. The birth and growth of children...

Where is my mother? No father blessed me in my infancy. Paradise lost. Adam came from God! I rather from Satan?

*Distressed, the CREATURE remembers something and finds FRANKENSTEIN's journal in the pocket of his coat. Terrified, he reads.*

'The Journal of Doctor Frankenstein.'

FRANKENSTEIN. Progress in the creation of... (*Stops.*)

CREATURE. Accursed creator, hateful day when I received life! God made man beautiful. My form is *filthy*!

> Did I request thee, Maker, from my clay
> To mould me man? Did I solicit thee
> From darkness to promote me?

*The music stops.*

AGATHA *wakes, kisses her father and exits.*

But these are kindly, gentle-mannered people…

*Another book.*

'Fable of the Lapdog and the Donkey.'

> The lapdog puts its paws upon its master's knee.
> The master strokes and kisses it; the love for all to see.
> Affection brings affection as its prize,
> The gentle donkey sees and tries likewise…

…Surely they will welcome me… surely.

*He plucks up courage and approaches the* OLD MAN.

Sir!

OLD MAN. Who is there?

CREATURE. Pardon. I am a traveller in want of rest.

OLD MAN. Please sit. Alas, my children are from home, and I am blind. I am afraid it will be difficult to find food for you.

CREATURE. Do not trouble, it is only kindness that I need.

OLD MAN. Where are you bound, friend?

CREATURE. I have no friend upon earth, nor yet relation. I am now going to claim the protection of some whom I sincerely love, and of whose favour I have some hopes, but a fatal prejudice against me clouds their eyes, and where they ought to see a feeling and kind friend, they may behold only a detestable monster.

OLD MAN. Misfortune indeed. Cannot you undeceive them?

CREATURE. That is the task I am about to undertake.

OLD MAN. I may perhaps be of help. I am blind, and cannot judge of your countenance, but there is something in your words which persuades me you are sincere. Where do these friends reside?

CREATURE. Near this spot.

OLD MAN. It will afford me true pleasure to assist another human being.

CREATURE. Thank you. From your lips first have I heard the voice of kindness.

OLD MAN. May I know their names and residence?

*The* CREATURE *pauses in indecision. The voices of* FELIX *and* SAFIE *are heard approaching.*

CREATURE. You and your family are the friends I seek. Do not desert me!

OLD MAN. Great God! Who are you?

*Enter* FELIX, SAFIE *and* AGATHA.

*They scream in terror and drag the* OLD MAN *out.*

SAFIE *flees but falls.*

*The* CREATURE *gently lifts her to her feet.*

FELIX *returns and attacks the* CREATURE *with the axe.*

*The* CREATURE *pushes* FELIX *off, throws down the axe, and watches innocently.*

FELIX *crosses to a chest and takes out a pistol. The* CREATURE *sees it as apparently offered, and comes closer to receive it.*

FELIX *laughs blackly, pulls the trigger and leaves.*

*The* CREATURE *cries in pain and grasps his shoulder. There is blood. To dull the pain he recites.*

CREATURE.
> Affection brings affection as its prize
> The gentle donkey sees and tries likewise.
> He lifts his hoof, brays, kisses master's cheek.
> His master beats him. Out vile beast! 'Tis bleak.

*Like a vandal, he smashes up the little settlement.*

Is there none among the myriad of men who will pity or assist me? War. I declare everlasting war against the species, and more than all, against him that formed me and sent me forth to this misery.

*He stares at the blood on his hands.*

## Scene Ten

*Enter* WILLIAM. *He stops.*

CREATURE. Surely this little creature is unprejudiced. He has lived too short a time to have imbibed a horror of deformity. If I can seize him, and educate him as my friend, I will not be so desolate in this peopled earth.

*He grabs hold of* WILLIAM, *who screams and struggles.*

Listen to me. I don't intend to hurt you.

WILLIAM. Let me go! Monster! Ugly wretch! You want to eat me. Let me go, or I'll tell my papa.

CREATURE. Boy, you will never see your father again. Come with me.

WILLIAM. I'll tell my papa. He is old Mr Frankenstein.

CREATURE. Frankenstein! So you belong to my enemy – to whom I have sworn eternal revenge.

WILLIAM. He will punish you. You dare not keep me…

CREATURE. You shall be my first victim.

*The* CREATURE *strangles* WILLIAM.

(*Reflecting.*) I too can create desolation.

*He sees the cameo around* WILLIAM's *neck.*

A most lovely woman… her dark eyes, fringed by deep lashes, and her lovely lips…

*He holds it against his face, sexually. Then rage returns.*

And I am forever deprived of the delights of such beautiful creatures.

*He turns to* FRANKENSTEIN.

Seeking a hiding place, I entered a barn. A girl was sleeping on the straw; not so beautiful as the portrait I held; but agreeable, and blooming in the loveliness of youth. I bent over her, and whispered, 'Awake, fairest, thy lover is near – he who would give his life for one affectionate look from thine eyes!'

She stirred. (*Conscience-stricken.*) Should she indeed awake, and see me, curse me, and denounce me a murderer? No. I committed the crime on the boy because I am robbed of all she might give me, of all... of all joy. She shall atone. The crime had its source in her: be hers the punishment! I bent over her, and placed the portrait deep in the folds of her dress.

For days I haunted that spot. Consumed by a burning passion, which only you can gratify.

I am alone; neither man nor woman will associate with me; but another as deformed and horrible as myself would not deny herself to me. My companion must be of the same species, and have the same defects. This being you must create.

FRANKENSTEIN *is dumbstruck.*

You must create a female for me. This you alone can do. I demand it of you as a right.

FRANKENSTEIN. I refuse, and no torture shall ever extort my consent.

Shall I create another like yourself, whose joint wickedness might desolate the world! Begone! I have answered you.

CREATURE. You are in the wrong. Have a care or I will work at your destruction, nor finish till I desolate your heart. But instead of threatening, I am content to reason with you.

*He speaks lightly and quickly.*

Everywhere I see bliss, from which I alone am excluded. I was benevolent and good – it was misery made me a fiend. Make me happy, and I shall again be virtuous.

What I ask is reasonable and moderate: a creature of another sex, but as hideous as myself. It is true we shall be monsters, cut off from the world; but on that account we shall be more attached to one another. Our lives may not be happy, but they will be harmless. Neither you, nor any human being shall ever see us again. We shall go to the vast wilds of South America. My food is not that of man; I do not destroy the flesh of animals to glut my appetite; acorns and berries suffice. My companion will be content with the same fare. We shall make our bed of dried leaves. The sun will shine on us and will ripen our food.

You have been pitiless. I now see compassion in your eyes.

Do not deny my request.

FRANKENSTEIN. You swear to be harmless; but haven't you already shown a malice that should reasonably make me distrust you?

CREATURE (*weary*). How inconstant are your feelings. (*Then very simply.*) My evil passions will have fled. My life will flow quietly. I shall feel affection, and be linked to the chain of existence, from which I am now excluded.

*Pause.*

FRANKENSTEIN. On your solemn oath, I will consent to your demand.

CREATURE. I swear by the sun, and by the blue sky of Heaven, and by the fire of love that burns my heart, that if you grant my prayer, you shall never behold me again.

Now depart and commence your labours: when you are ready, I shall appear.

*End of Act One.*

## ACT TWO

### Scene Eleven

*Geneva.*

FATHER (*with brilliant perception*). Victor, you are not well.

> It is this gloom of mind I wish to dissipate. I have been lost
> as to its cause; but yesterday an idea struck me. Your
> engagement to Elizabeth...

FRANKENSTEIN (*stopping him*). Father, I love my cousin
tenderly and sincerely. My future hopes are entirely bound in
the expectation of our union.

FATHER. Then we shall proceed to an immediate marriage.

> ELIZABETH *is silent.*

FRANKENSTEIN (*awkwardly*). Father, I should like to travel,
and see the world before sitting down for life in my native
town. I should like to visit... England!

FATHER. England? England!

> FATHER *laughs.*

HENRY. I shall come with you, Victor.

FATHER. I am content. The amusements of travelling will
restore your tranquillity, and the wedding will take place
immediately on your return.

> *He exits.*

ELIZABETH (*almost defeated*). We all depend upon you,
Victor, and if you are miserable what must be our feelings?

> *She exits.*

FRANKENSTEIN (*to the audience*). Discoveries have been made in England which are indispensable to my success. (*Irritable*.) I cannot compose a female without profound and laborious study.

*Lights change.*

**Scene Twelve**

HENRY. We descend the Rhine by boat.

FRANKENSTEIN. Woman...

HENRY. A singularly variegated landscape, with a charm I never saw equalled. We travel at harvest time.

FRANKENSTEIN. The gathering of necessary parts.

HENRY. Listen! The song of the vineyard labourers.

FRANKENSTEIN. Femur, tibia, fibula, patella, tarsal, metatarsal.

HENRY. We glide downstream to Cologne, then across the plains of Holland.

FRANKENSTEIN. A slightly wider pelvis.

HENRY. Rotterdam. I stand in the prow!

FRANKENSTEIN. Sternum, clavicle, sacrum.

HENRY. This is what it is to live! Now I enjoy existence.

FRANKENSTEIN. It is the torture of single drops of water continually falling on the head.

HENRY. And the open sea. October. I first see the white cliffs of England.

FRANKENSTEIN. Complexion.

HENRY. The banks of the Thames are flat.

FRANKENSTEIN. Form.

HENRY. Gravesend… The Tower… St Paul's… Joyous, busy faces!

FRANKENSTEIN. Eyes, nose, ears.

HENRY. Inexhaustible differences of manners!

FRANKENSTEIN. Liver, pancreas, intestines.

HENRY. Oxford.

FRANKENSTEIN. Brain.

HENRY (*bliss*). Oxford! The colleges, ancient and picturesque, and the lovely river Isis flowing through verdant meadows.

FRANKENSTEIN. Her heart.

HENRY. Embosomed in ancient trees. Too short! We leave with regret.

FRANKENSTEIN. Spleen.

HENRY. For the little town of Matlock. We visit the wondrous cave, its cabinets of natural history, with the curiosities displayed.

FRANKENSTEIN. Womb, cervix, vagina. I am a blasted tree. The bolt has entered my soul.

HENRY. Victor! Cumberland and Westmorland.

FRANKENSTEIN (*relief*). Lungs.

HENRY. Look at the sky, Victor! Blue… cloudless… and the sun!

FRANKENSTEIN (*grief*). Tranquillity.

*Beat.*

HENRY. Edinburgh.

FRANKENSTEIN (*stopping him*). Henry…

HENRY. I like Edinburgh but not so well as Oxford. Then St Andrews, and the fair city of Perth…

FRANKENSTEIN. Henry, I wish to make the tour of Scotland alone. Do you enjoy yourself, and let this city be our rendezvous. I may be absent a month or two. I entreat you, leave me to peace and solitude. And when I return, I hope it will be with a lighter heart, more congenial to your own temper.

HENRY. I had rather be with you in your solitary rambles, than with these Scotch people. Hasten to return, that I may again feel myself at home, which I cannot do in your absence. (*Puzzled.*) And where on earth are you going?

FRANKENSTEIN. I am fixed on one of the remotest of the Orkneys.

*Thunderous waves.*

**Scene Thirteen**

*Orkney.*

FRANKENSTEIN *works alone for quite a long time.*

*The female is nearly complete.*

*The* CREATURE *slips into the space. He watches.*

*The waves fade.* FRANKENSTEIN *speaks without looking at the* CREATURE.

FRANKENSTEIN (*quiet*). Three years ago I was engaged like this. I created a fiend, whose unparalleled barbarity has desolated my heart. I am now about to animate another, of whose dispositions I am ignorant; she might become ten times more malignant than he, and delight in murder and wretchedness. He has sworn to hide himself in the deserts, but she has not; she may refuse to comply with an agreement made before her creation. They may even hate each other. The creature who already lives loathes his own deformity.

Might he not conceive an even greater abhorrence when it comes before his eyes in female form? She also may turn from him in disgust; she may quit him, and he be again alone, deserted by his own species.

*The* CREATURE *crosses and clutches the shrouded female figure in a close embrace.*

Even if they leave Europe, and inhabit the deserts of the new world, one result will be children, and a race of devils be propagated to threaten the very existence of man. Have I the right for my own benefit, to inflict this curse upon everlasting generations? I shudder to think it. Future ages might curse me, as my selfishness buys my own peace at the price of the whole human race.

To create another like you would be an act of the most atrocious selfishness.

The wickedness of my promise bursts upon me.

CREATURE. I come to claim the fulfilment of your promise.

FRANKENSTEIN. I am helpless, as in a frightful dream, when in vain you try to flee from danger, and are rooted to the spot.

CREATURE. What do you intend? Will you destroy the work you have done? Do you dare break your promise? I have endured cold and misery, incalculable fatigue and hunger. Do you dare destroy my hopes?

FRANKENSTEIN *destroys the figure. He breaks its neck.*

FRANKENSTEIN. I do break my promise. Never will I create another.

CREATURE. Shall each man find a wife for his bosom and I be alone?

I have reasoned with you, but you have proved unworthy. Remember that I have power. I can make you so wretched that the light of day will be hateful to you. You are my creator, but I am your master. Obey!

FRANKENSTEIN. Your threats cannot move me to do an act of wickedness.

*The* CREATURE *curses* FRANKENSTEIN.

CREATURE. Man, beware! You may hate; but your hours will pass in dread and misery, and soon the bolt will fall which must ravish your happiness for ever. You may blast my other passions; but revenge remains – revenge, henceforth dearer than light or food. I may die; but first you, my tyrant and tormentor, shall curse the sun, that gazes on your misery. Beware; for I am fearless. I will watch with the wiliness of a snake, that I may sting with its venom. Man, you shall repent of the injuries you inflict. I go!

*He moves to exit, then speaks quietly.*

And remember this: I shall be with you on your wedding night.

FRANKENSTEIN. Villain! Before you sign my death warrant, be sure you are yourself safe.

*The* CREATURE *exits.*

'I will be with you on your wedding night.' So that is the fulfilment of my destiny. In that hour I will die, and at once satisfy and extinguish his malice. So be it.

*He begins to tidy, and lifts a medical chest towards a little boat. He pulls aside the tarpaulin. He retches in shock and weeps. The audience do not see the body. Only a hand.*

You followed me! And now have my murderous machinations deprived you also of life? You, my friend, my benefactor. Has this gentle and lovely being perished for ever? Can you now only exist in my memory?

I am the murderer of William, of Justine… and of Henry Clerval.

Why do *I* not die? Death snatches away so many children, the only hopes of their doting parents; and how many youthful lovers, one day in the bloom of health and hope, are the next a prey for worms and the grave! Of what materials am I made, that I can resist so many shocks, which, like the turning of the wheel, continually renew the torture?

I am doomed to live!

FRANKENSTEIN *exits, and the* CREATURE *follows closely.*

## Scene Fourteen

*Geneva.*

ELIZABETH (*uncomprehending*). We shall see you restored to health, Victor.

FRANKENSTEIN *is silent.*

ELIZABETH. Poor Henry. Cousin, you have suffered...

FRANKENSTEIN. If 'he' were vanquished, I should be a free man. But what freedom, Elizabeth, what freedom? Such as the peasant enjoys when his family have been massacred before his eyes? When his dwelling has been burnt, his lands laid waste, and he is adrift penniless and alone, but free? Such would be my liberty. Except that – (*Looking at her uncertainly.*) I possess a treasure.

ELIZABETH. Victor, we were childhood playfellows and as we have grown older we have been valued friends. But a lively affection may not always promise... a more intimate union.

FRANKENSTEIN. Elizabeth.

ELIZABETH. Victor, it is your happiness I desire. Your free choice.

FRANKENSTEIN. Sweet, beloved Elizabeth. Softened feelings whisper of paradise. But the apple is already eaten.

ELIZABETH. Victor…

FRANKENSTEIN. I would die to make you happy.

ELIZABETH. In my airy future dreams you are always my companion.

FRANKENSTEIN. To you I consecrate my life. I love you and look forward to our marriage.

ELIZABETH. Then be happy. There is nothing to distress you.

FRANKENSTEIN (*shouting*). Father, Father!

ELIZABETH. Something whispers to me, whispers… But I will not listen to such a sinister voice. Victor, look at the clouds, which sometimes obscure and sometimes rise above Mont Blanc. Look also at the fish… innumerable… swimming in the waters. We can distinguish every pebble. On this divine day, nature appears happy.

*Their embrace is passionate, needy, incomplete.*

FRANKENSTEIN. Elizabeth, I have one secret. A dreadful one. It will chill your frame with horror. I will confide it to you the day after our marriage. But until then…

ELIZABETH. Victor…

FRANKENSTEIN. Shh! Until then, I conjure you, do not mention or allude to it. (*Calling.*) Father!

*Enter* FATHER.

Let the day be fixed.

FATHER. Heavy misfortunes have befallen us. Let us only cling closer to what remains.

*Exit* FATHER *and* ELIZABETH. FRANKENSTEIN *loads a pistol.*

FRANKENSTEIN. And on that day I will consecrate myself to the happiness of Elizabeth… with my life or with my death.

*He turns to the audience.*

These were the last moments during which I enjoyed the feeling of hope.

I took every precaution to protect myself. I thought I only prepared my own death.

*We hear faint wedding music.* FATHER *is ecstatic.*

FATHER (*off*). Welcome… welcome… hallo… thank you so much… thank you… hallo…

FRANKENSTEIN *cocks a pistol.*

FRANKENSTEIN. But as if possessed of magic powers the monster blinded me.

*A scream from* ELIZABETH. *A sexual cry from the* CREATURE.

*The* CREATURE *is sitting on* ELIZABETH's *body. Her upper half is covered by her dress. Elsewhere, her disembodied head.*

Mine has been a tale of horrors, Captain Walton. I have reached their acme.

FRANKENSTEIN's FATHER *looks at his son.* FRANKENSTEIN *exits.*

FATHER *has the beginnings of a fit.*

*Lights change.*

**Scene Fifteen**

*The ship.*

FRANKENSTEIN. My father of course could not live under the horrors accumulated round him; an apoplectic fit was brought on and in a few days he died in my arms.

During many months they called me mad. But I awakened to reason, and at the same time to revenge, the only and devouring passion of my soul. It has kept me alive – just. I have pursued him, this long, long while across the blue Mediterranean, the Black Sea, the wilds of Tartary and Russia. Although he still evades me, I ever follow in his track. I have traversed the sea of ice.

WALTON. Then such a monster really has existence. I cannot doubt it; yet I am lost in wonder at his 'formation'. How did you...?

FRANKENSTEIN (*drily*). I see by your eagerness, my friend, and the hope which your eyes express, that you expect to be informed of the secret. That cannot be. I will not lead you on, unguarded and ardent, as I was, to your destruction and infallible misery. Learn from my example how dangerous is the acquirement of knowledge.

I believed myself destined for some great enterprise. I trod heaven in my power, I burned with the idea. And how am I sunk.

WALTON. I have so longed for a friend, one who would sympathise with me and love me. And now on these desert seas I have found one; but I fear I have gained him only to know his value and lose him. I would reconcile him to life...

FRANKENSTEIN. Thank you, Captain Walton, but when you speak of new ties and fresh affections, do you think any can replace those who are gone? Can any man be to me as Henry was; or any woman another Elizabeth? The companions of our childhood always possess a certain power over our minds, which no later friend can obtain. (*Wryly.*) They know our infantile dispositions.

*Enter the* CREW.

WALTON. Officer?

CREWMAN. Captain, we have been chosen to come in deputation.

WALTON. Proceed.

CREWMAN. The men fear, sir, if the ice should dissipate, and a free passage be opened, that you may be rash enough to continue the voyage and lead us into fresh dangers. They insist, therefore, that you engage with a solemn promise that if the vessel should be freed from the ice you will instantly direct course southward.

WALTON. There is something terrible, appalling in our situation, yet my hopes do not desert me...

FRANKENSTEIN (*to* CREW). What do you demand of your captain? Are you so easily turned from your design? Did you not call this a glorious expedition? And why was it glorious? Not because the way was placid as a southern sea, but because danger and death surrounded it, and these you were to brave and overcome, for honour and the good of all mankind. And now, with the first imaginings, do you shrink away, not strong enough? 'Poor souls, they were chilly and returned to their firesides.' You needn't have come this far, and dragged your Captain to the shame of defeat, merely to prove yourselves cowards. Oh, be steady to your purposes. Do not return to your families with the stigma of disgrace. This ice is not made of such stuff as your hearts may be.

The ice cannot withstand you if you say it shall not.

*Beat.*

WALTON (*to* CREW). I hope you will consider what has been said. And that, with reflection, your courage may revive.

*Silence. The* CREW *are implacable.*

*Agonised,* WALTON *turns to* FRANKENSTEIN *and back to the* CREW.

If we are not destroyed, I consent to return.

*The* CREW *exit, shouting and cheering.*

The die is cast. Thus are my hopes...

FRANKENSTEIN (*quietly mocking*). Bravo, Captain…

WALTON. Frankenstein, the lives of all these men are endangered through me.

FRANKENSTEIN *does not reply.*

If we are lost, my mad schemes are the cause. I must return.

FRANKENSTEIN. Do so, if you will; but I will not. You may give up your purpose. Mine is assigned to me by Heaven. And yet I have failed. I am weak; the strength I relied on is gone. I must die and he is still in being.

Swear to me, Walton, that he shall not escape, that you will seek him, that he shall not triumph. Thrust your sword into his heart.

(*Confused.*) But dare I ask you to do this, when I may be misled by passion, or already disturbed by death?

In a fit of enthusiastic madness I created a rational creature. I was bound to him, for his well-being. This was my duty. But there were other duties paramount…

*Enter* JUSTINE *silently.*

…duties towards my own species, because they embraced a greater happiness or misery.

*Enter* ELIZABETH *and* FATHER.

That he should live troubles me. Yet in other respects, this moment of release is my only happy one for several years. The forms of the beloved dead flit before me and I hasten to their arms.

*Enter* WILLIAM.

Farewell, Walton. Seek happiness in tranquillity and – (*He laughs bitterly.*) avoid ambition, even if only the apparently innocent one of distinguishing yourself in science or discoveries.

Ha! But why do I say this? Though I have been blasted in these hopes, another may succeed.

*A sound makes* WALTON *turn away. The* CREATURE *appears. When* WALTON *turns back,* FRANKENSTEIN *has died.*

CREATURE (*calmly*). That is also my victim. The thread of my being is wound to its close. Oh, Frankenstein, what does it serve that now I ask you to pardon me? Alas, he is cold, he cannot answer me.

WALTON. Your repentance is superfluous. If you had listened to the voice of conscience, Frankenstein would still be living.

CREATURE (*appalled*). Do you *dream*? Do you think I have been dead to remorse? Do you think the groans of Henry Clerval were music to my ears? My heart was poisoned with remorse. (*Turning to* FRANKENSTEIN.) I was susceptible to love and sympathy. I pitied Frankenstein.

*The* CREATURE *is faced by all his victims.* ELIZABETH *is with* FRANKENSTEIN.

But when I saw that he dared to hope for happiness, for passions from which I was barred, then envy filled me, filled me with vengeance. I was the slave, not the master, of an impulse I could not disobey. Evil became my good.

And now it is ended. There is my last victim.

WALTON. Hypocritical wretch! You throw a torch into a pile of buildings; and when they are consumed in flames you sit among the ruins and lament the fall to me.

CREATURE. Oh, no. I seek no fellow-feeling in my misery. What sympathy should I seek? Once I hoped to meet beings who, pardoning my outward form, would love me for the qualities I unfolded. But now crime has degraded me. Virtue has become a shadow, the fallen angel a malignant devil.

Yet even the devil, in his desolation, had friends; I am quite alone.

*He is face to face with* WILLIAM.

Misery made me malicious.

*The* CREW *has lit torches.*

Perhaps you hate me; but your abhorrence cannot equal that with which I regard myself. Do not fear that I shall work future mischief. No man's death is needed now. Except my own.

And do not think I shall be slow.

I shall quit this vessel on the ice-raft which brought me, and shall seek the most northern extremity of the globe; I shall collect my funeral pile and consume to ashes this miserable frame. I shall no longer be the prey of feelings unsatisfied, unquenched.

He is dead who called me into being, and when I am no more, the very remembrance of us both will vanish.

Light, feeling, and sense will pass away; and in this must I find my happiness. Long ago, when I first saw the sun and the stars, and felt the winds play on my cheeks, and these were all to me, I should have wept to die; now it is my only consolation. Frankenstein, blasted as you were, my agony was still superior to yours; for the sting of remorse will not cease to rankle in my wounds, until death closes them for ever, and my ashes are swept into the sea.

Then my spirit will sleep in peace. (*Suddenly hard and bitter.*) Or if it thinks, it will surely not think thus.

*He exits.*

ELIZABETH. Man, how ignorant you are in your pride of wisdom. Cease. You know not what it is you say.

*The End.*

**Other Adaptations in this Series**

ANIMAL FARM
Ian Wooldridge
*Adapted from* George Orwell

ANNA KARENINA
Helen Edmundson
*Adapted from* Leo Tolstoy

ARTHUR & GEORGE
David Edgar
*Adapted from* Julian Barnes

THE CANTERBURY TALES
Mike Poulton
*Adapted from* Geoffrey Chaucer

A CHRISTMAS CAROL
Karen Louise Hebden
*Adapted from* Charles Dickens

CORAM BOY
Helen Edmundson
*Adapted from* Jamila Gavin

DAVID COPPERFIELD
Alastair Cording
*Adapted from* Charles Dickens

DR JEKYLL AND MR HYDE
David Edgar
*Adapted from* Robert Louis Stevenson

DRACULA
Liz Lochhead
*Adapted from* Bram Stoker

EMMA
Martin Millar and Doon MacKichan
*Adapted from* Jane Austen

FAR FROM THE MADDING CROWD
Mark Healy
*Adapted from* Thomas Hardy

FAUSTUS
Rupert Goold and Ben Power
*After* Christopher Marlowe

GREAT EXPECTATIONS
Nick Ormerod and Declan Donnellan
*Adapted from* Charles Dickens

HIS DARK MATERIALS
Nicholas Wright
*Adapted from* Philip Pullman

JANE EYRE
Polly Teale
*Adapted from* Charlotte Brontë

THE JUNGLE BOOK
Stuart Paterson
*Adapted from* Rudyard Kipling

KES
Lawrence Till
*Adapted from* Barry Hines

MADAME BOVARY
Fay Weldon
*Adapted from* Gustave Flaubert

MARY BARTON
Rona Munro
*Adapted from* Elizabeth Gaskell

THE MILL ON THE FLOSS
Helen Edmundson
*Adapted from* George Eliot

NORTHANGER ABBEY
Tim Luscombe
*Adapted from* Jane Austen

NOUGHTS & CROSSES
Dominic Cooke
*Adapted from* Malorie Blackman

PERSUASION
Mark Healy
*Adapted from* Jane Austen

THE RAGGED TROUSERED
    PHILANTHROPISTS
Howard Brenton
*Adapted from* Robert Tressell

THE RAILWAY CHILDREN
Mike Kenny
*Adapted from* E. Nesbit

SENSE AND SENSIBILITY
Mark Healy
*Adapted from* Jane Austen

SLEEPING BEAUTY
Rufus Norris

SUNSET SONG
Alastair Cording
*Adapted from* Lewis Grassic Gibbon

TREASURE ISLAND
Stuart Paterson
*Adapted from* Robert Louis Stevenson

WAR AND PEACE
Helen Edmundson
*Adapted from* Leo Tolstoy